RALPH CUF

IN PRO FOOTBALL BLACK QUARTERBACKS AND THE N-WORD MATTERS

THE ACCEPTANCE OF THE BLACK QUARTERBACK
AND THE BLACK MALE IN SOCIETY

outskirts
press

In Pro Football Black Quarterbacks and the N-Word Matters
The Acceptance of the Black Quarterback and the Black Male in Society
All Rights Reserved.
Copyright © 2018 Ralph Cuffeea Allsopp
v4.0 r1.1

The opinions expressed in this manuscript are solely the opinions of the author and do not represent the opinions or thoughts of the publisher. The author has represented and warranted full ownership and/or legal right to publish all the materials in this book.

This book may not be reproduced, transmitted, or stored in whole or in part by any means, including graphic, electronic, or mechanical without the express written consent of the publisher except in the case of brief quotations embodied in critical articles and reviews.

Outskirts Press, Inc.
http://www.outskirtspress.com

Paperback ISBN: 978-1-4787-9009-9
Hardback ISBN: 978-1-9772-1305-1

Cover Photo © 2018 Ralph Cuffeea Allsopp. All rights reserved - used with permission.

Outskirts Press and the "OP" logo are trademarks belonging to Outskirts Press, Inc.

PRINTED IN THE UNITED STATES OF AMERICA

*Homage and appreciation to
Alicia Garza, Opal Tometi, and Patrisse Cullors.*

Because Black pro quarterbacks don't matter, and Black portrayals in the media don't matter, unless "Black Lives Matter"

*To the full-grown, full-blown, fire-breathing Black women in my life: Grandmother May, Mother Lillian,
daughter Whitney Jackson, and my colleagues Adrienn Griffin, Carol Webster, Sherryl Browne Graves, Eloise Archibald, Sharon Hobbs, Kamala Motti, Janice Bennet, Audrey Murrell and Jacqueline Bursch*

Dedicated to Black quarterbacks (BQBs) Fritz Pollard, Warren Moon, Condredge Holloway, and Randall Cunningham.

*Finally, in memory of Dr. Adrienn Griffin, my half-back buddy Salvatore Saroka , Betty Jenkins, my brothers
"Butch" Joseph Allsopp and Carl Edward Allsopp*

TABLE OF CONTENTS

The Black Quarterback and the Black Male in Society 1
Sports and Gender-Racial Stereotypes in Sports 4
Warren Moon 10
Vincent Young 17
Steve McNair 18
Joe Gilliam 20
Michael Vick 23
Randall Cunningham 26
The N-Word Matters! 29
The Black Quarterback Social Change TimeLine 32
TimeLine of Social Change and the Changes in Football 42
Black Youth Racism and Sports 53
Bibliography 69

THE BLACK QUARTERBACK AND THE BLACK MALE IN SOCIETY

IN THE LATE 1970s, this writer sought to explore the relationship between the Black quarterbacks in the NFL and the Black male in society. My unpublished paper, "The Black Quarterback as a Product of Social Change," was cited in the published article "Causal Attributions of Performance for Black and White Quarterbacks in the NFL: A Look at the Sports Pages" (A. J. Murrell and E. M. Curtis, *Journal of Sport and Social Issues*, August 1, 1994).

Although consistent with my thesis, it was beyond my imagination to think that the emergence of Black quarterbacks in the NFL and Black males in society would rise to the level of an African-American's election as the president of the United States (2008). Obviously, the position of quarterback is by no means the equivalent of being president, but ironically, the same racial slurs incurred by the first professional Black quarterbacks were similar to those directed at the first Black president. The quarterback position provides leadership, calls the plays, and receives too much credit for success and an inordinate amount of criticism for failure. The president, likewise, provides leadership and calls the plays for the nation, and he is highly praised and/or severely criticized for his perceived successes and failures.

This inquiry focuses on the psychological cost of achieving success in a position that historically is considered "whites only," like the restrooms and water fountains of the Jim Crow era.

In the previous paper, I composed a list of Black quarterbacks, which included Fritz Pollard (1920), George Talliaferro (1949), and Willie Thrower (1953), who played in the fifties; and Marlin Briscoe (1968), "Jefferson Street" Joe Gilliam (1973), Warren Moon (Canadian Football League 1974, NFL 1984, CFL Hall of Fame 2000, NFL Hall of Fame 2006), Doug Williams (1974), Condredge Holloway (CFL 1975 CFL, CFL Hall of Fame 1999), James Harris (1975), and Matt Reed (1976), who played in the sixties and seventies.

Jeff Blake (1992), Randall Cunningham (1985), Tony Banks (1994), Steve McNair (1995), Kordell Stewart (1995), Daunte Culpepper (1999), Charlie Batch (1999), Aaron Brooks (1999), Shaun King (1999), Michael Bishop (1999), and Akili Smith (1999) all played in the nineties.

In the 2000s, there are Antonio Wright (200), Quincy Carter (2001), Michael Vick (2001), Vince Young (2006), Jason Campbell (2006), Robert Griffin III (2012), Russell Wilson (2012), Colin Kaepernick (2011), Cameron Newton (2011), Tyrod Taylor (2011), James Lanaed Winston (2015), and Dak Prescott (2016).

Achieving the status of professional quarterback does not

scratch the surface of the psychological trauma these Black men endured to obtain this goal, not unlike a Black male seeking the position of President of the United States. Unlike President Obama, many Black quarterbacks fail under the pressure of this extreme notoriety and criticism.

As someone who has studied psychology (and minored in philosophy and sociology), this writer wanted to look at the political, sociological, and psychological landscape that produces these athletes. Sports psychologists need to understand, react, and be proactive with athletes of color as they pursue their dreams of success in sport and life. It is necessary to understand the impact of social and sports stereotypes that accrue to athletes, particularly Black (male and female) athletes, as they mentally and physically develop into the heroes and superheroes in the realm of sports. This writer also wanted to highlight the pitfalls that hasten Black quarterbacks' fall from grace.

Since the end of Reconstruction and the subsequent emergence of the Jim Crow laws, African-Americans have struggled to shed themselves of the racial stereotypes bestowed on them to justify the reason for their enslavement: stupid, apelike, violent, animal instinct, undependable, superstitious, and simple-minded. The Black man was an animal with a big body and a small brain as opposed to his European counterpart with a great mind and a serviceable body. These beliefs have resulted in preventing Blacks from flying fighter planes, being in combat positions in the armed services, participating in certain sports, and being restricted to certain positions which do not require thinking, planning, or organization.

SPORTS AND GENDER-RACIAL STEREOTYPES IN SPORTS

BOXER JACK JOHNSON, Black heavyweight champion of the world (1908–1915), was the embodiment of all the fears and stereotypes Whites had about Black men. The Black quarterback later became the symbol of all the stereotypes attributed to the Black male. Hence, when we talk about the Black quarterback, we are really talking about the Black race, which is why Black quarterbacks matter. Jack Johnson was arrogant, outspoken, and rambunctious. He consorted with White women and flaunted his Blackness every chance he got. He was usually a front-page item in Black and White newspapers alike. There was a national effort to find "The Great White Hope" who would defeat Johnson and put him on his black ass, where he and his race belonged. Flash forward to O. J. Simpson, who seemed like the antithesis of Jack Johnson. He was good looking, fair-skinned, educated, and articulate. His easy smile, soft voice, and movie-star appearance went against the stereotype. He was not just another black buck. He was not violent, and he could be trusted with White women. O. J. was okay; there was no issue with him consorting with White women and later marrying a White woman. Unfortunately, O. J. Simpson became the ultimate betrayer. It was as if Shakespeare's *Othello* was playing out before our very eyes; a jealous Black man kills his estranged White wife, Nicole Simpson, and her White friend, Andrew Goldman. Jack Johnson and O. J. reinforced the stereotypes created during the slave trade and that continue to this day. It is possible to see professional sports as a system that controls and manipulates the status and image of Black people. Sports organizations were similar to the agricultural system of the early South. Both systems were male-dominated institutions, which controlled Blacks for purposes of economic gain. Both systems had implicit/explicit beliefs and myths that manipulated and stigmatized Blacks.

Plantation owners determined how athletic (boxing) contests were organized, who the players were, and what the rewards would be. They would select two of their biggest, brawniest, and blackest bucks and toss them in a makeshift ring. The masters would guzzle gallons of whiskey and rum, crack jokes, and make big wagers while the two bucks beat each other to a bloody pulp. For inflicting severe injuries and perhaps even death on each other the bucks might get a little better food, an extra set of hand-me-downs and, if especially lucky, their freedom. These Black bucks were their master's prized gladiators. They had to be treated "a little special" (Hutchinson, 1994, 35). The motion pictures *Django Unchained* (2012) and *Mandingo* (1976) vividly depict these contests.

More importantly, the slave owner realized all the profits

and entertainment from these early athletic (fighting) contests. As important as the entertainment and economic aspects were, the plantation owners also reaped psychological benefits. These athletic contests allowed the owners to control both the physical and psychological behaviors of the enslaved athletes. In addition, they could decrease their fear of the Black male and act out their fantasies and fear of the Black male, the Black female and the White female.

The myth was that Blacks were similar to primates because of their color and their African heritage. Logically, this belief extended to the idea that primates (Blacks) were interior to humans (Whites), intellectually and psychologically.

Along with this forced association with primates, Black males had an animal nature and a bestial sexual desire. This became the excuse that allowed White males to express their own sexual nature. With the Black slave representing the negative sexual aspects of human behavior, the White slave owner was free to act out his sexuality without guilt. Because of his religious underpinnings, wanton sexuality was taboo, and sexuality was the province of White males. Only the slave owner had the power to express his sexuality and forcibly seduce the Black female, while at the same time keeping the White female pure and away from anything sexual. The White male could also keep his guilt and anxiety controlled by believing that the Black male wanted to seduce/rape White women. This self-created fantasy/fear further created the need to control the male. The sexually gifted Black male was the biological complement to the sexually and physically endowed Black female.

The White male would have fantasies about the superhuman

power of the Black male. He had the extraordinary powers needed to satisfy the Black female. Such thoughts could engender both a sense of admiration and fear, and out of fear, the need to control. The psychological need to control the Black male's sexuality enabled the slave master to contain his guilt by projecting his negative sexual feelings/behaviors on the Black male. White males controlled Black males' freedom to have sex with Black females, not only for boxing and plantation work, but also when the Black female came of age, the first person she had to have sex with was her White slave master.

The Black athlete's image also is manipulated and controlled. Sports organizations are the control mechanism, with White males clustered at the top and the majority of the relatively well-paid Black athletes at the bottom. By comparing the old antebellum plantation system with today's megacomplex system of professional sports, the basic negative images still persist and continue to serve the need for control. Society accumulates a great deal of ideas, values, and information about Blacks from seeing them portrayed on television and in other types of media. There is research (Greenberg, 1973) suggesting that Whites seem to be more influenced by media portrayals than by actual contact with other ethnic groups. The image of Blacks in sports, interviews, criminal trials, the nightly news, sitcoms, etc. is how society expects Blacks to be and to behave. Society seems more comfortable when its personal contact confirms the stereotype of a positive nature and is less at ease, but not surprised, when the actual contact with Black athletes confirms the negative stereotypes present in books, television, movies, newspapers, or on the internet. The media should educate, inform, and be truthful in order to break the negative chains of continued subjugation and vilification of the image of Black athletes and Black males in general.

Among other factors, contact sports provide an outlet for individuals who are prone to use aggression as a problem-solving technique. Football, hockey, and, to a lesser extent, basketball have given a select group of individuals (Black and White) a license to express their aggression in socially accepted ways and be rewarded for it. The males of any race may be most associated with displaying violence and aggression. Sports, such as football, hockey, and, to a lesser extent, basketball, may attract individuals who have not found other appropriate outlets to express their feelings of anger and their penchant for violence. Sports give male and female athletes the license to express their feelings, but it also ensures that they can and will be compensated financially for it. Fame and fortune are powerful motivators to pursue sports if one has the physical skills and talent. This book attempts to illuminate the price and toll that racist stereotypes take on the Black athlete in terms of his or her self-concept and emotional well-being, and how they relate to the laws of society, player-fan interactions, player-media interactions, player-coach interactions, and their family, wives, and children. It seems that, on a daily basis, the media tells us of the high incidence of violent interpersonal relationships and possibly no viable relationships in the lives of White/Black males and White/Black athletes.

The nasty little secret is many athletes (Black and White) have a penchant to solve problems by taking action, not by talking and negotiating. It seems to be a biological imperative that the men have to marshal their creative (aggressive) energies by creating physical solutions to problems. Women, on the other hand, find greater comfort in talking about their problems, lowering their level of anxiety and conflict. (Gray, 1992) The hunter-gatherer instinct of males makes them want to "just do it!" When it is third and four, this is not the time to talk; it is time to act.

Whatever the conflict or sports situation, there comes a time when athletes, male or female, must assert mental and physical control over their world. There is that little boy or girl inside that says, "I want what I want, and I will access every fiber of my body to get it." They use their well-trained bodies to achieve their sports goals. Unfortunately, these aggressive problem-solving strategies are ill advised and inappropriate in everyday (non-sports) interpersonal relationships.

Perhaps motivated by the infamous O. J. Simpson trial (1994) and the 911 tapes of the Juice terrorizing his then-wife Nicole Simpson, *Sports Illustrated* devoted a story about top athletes who have used physical force to resolve their personal conflicts. Far too often, these athletes are Black: O. J. Simpson, Barry Bonds, Mike Tyson, Daryl Strawberry, and Robert Parish, to name a few who enhanced the myth of the (Black) male athlete being a passionate but violent figure.

WARREN MOON

FORMER BLACK QUARTERBACK Warren Moon is a winner of the NFL's "Man of the Year" award, a Hall of Famer, and founder of a clinic for Houston's disadvantaged children. Moon also was allegedly caught in this web of domestic violence. Previously, the public's heart went out to him when they learned he was receiving death threats and weathering a daily cry of "Nigger, go home." This was not merely because he was suffering a high number of interceptions and his team was plummeting from playoff contention. Perhaps fans still carried memories of Moon losing a previous playoff game when the Buffalo Bills rebounded from the greatest playoff deficit in history to beat the Houston Oilers. Were the fans seeing Moon as impotent? Did they see him as someone who could pass well but not consistently? Someone who did not have the emotional stability or mental toughness of a Joe Montana in order to rally himself and his team in the face of extreme adversity? Even before the Buffalo game,

Moon was receiving death threats. During a 1990 game with the Cleveland Browns, Houston's Director of Security Grady Sessums led a squad of local police that surrounded Moon, saying to him, "There's been a threat on your life...And there are reasons to believe this is credible." In his book, *Never Give Up on Your Dream* (2009), Moon seemed to minimize the significance of these threats by suggesting that fans were placing inordinate importance on football; after all, it is just a game.

It seemed that Moon was emotionally living in a bubble. Warren Moon must have been aware of other Black athletes who were the first African-Americans in their sports, such as Jackie Robinson breaking the color line in baseball (1947). In 1944, Robinson preceded Rosa Parks in refusing to give up his seat and move to the back of the bus at Fort Hood, Georgia. Instead of Robinson launching the civil rights movement, the army court-martialed him. Perhaps Mr. Moon may not have known of Jerry LeVias (SMU, 1965), a former Houston Oiler (1969). LeVias was the first Black athlete to integrate the Southwest Conference, and yes, his life was threatened on and off the football field. They would shoot him if he played another game. Perhaps Moon did not know about Fritz Pollard (1920), George Talliaferro (194), Willie Thrower (1953), Marlin Briscoe (1968), or Joe Gilliam (1972), all predecessors to the Black quarterback position in the NFL. These men undoubtedly were called the N-word, and undoubtedly, all of them had their lives threatened. Everybody knows it was not because of a game called football. It was about *racism*, about them daring to cross the "Jim Crow line" and becoming quarterbacks in the NFL. They quickly learned that the NFL quarterback position was like a water fountain with a sign that read "Whites only." Warren Moon, off the field, was still a nice person and a man. He was not the straw man, the bogeyman, who should be killed because he was destroying the purity of the quarterback position. Warren Moon had a lovely wife and fine children, and his socially conscious charitable works were well recognized. When Moon was traded to the Minnesota Vikings, it seemed to be a great move for his family and his football career. It was there that he began working under Dennis Green, the second Black head coach in the national Football League. It seemed Moon's only difficulty would be adjusting to an offense that did not feature the shotgun formation.

Apparently, however, the tranquility within the Moon household and within him was unraveling. Let us remember that Warren Moon was not drafted by the NFL due to what many thought was the league's belief that African-Americans could not be effective quarterbacks. Finally, when he was invited into the NFL, many football fans eviscerated him and his race when he was not meeting their expectations. Moon writes in his book (Moon and Yeager, 2009) that he wanted to be seen as a quarterback and not as a Black quarterback. The sad truth is that society sees everyone first by the color of his or her skin, and you have to rise above it. Back in the day, many whites did not see the "Brown Bomber" as being Black because he single-handedly destroyed the German threat, Max Scheming, in the boxing ring, thus symbolically defeating Germany. In other words, Joe Louis earned his personhood; he earned his celebrity. He was (temporarily) seen as the world heavyweight champion, not just another Black boxer. Warren Moon, in the eyes of the fans, had not earned his designation as a quarterback in America (as he had done in Canada); therefore, no matter how he saw himself, he was treated as a Black man trying to play quarterback. On his good days in Houston, he was accepted; on his bad days, he was just another nigger and was labeled as such. With the support of his wife, Moon seemed to be holding it together. He was dealing with the fickleness of society, whose attacks appeared to have penetrated his psyche and became his inner demons. If that were true, he would not have been the first, nor unfortunately the last, Black man or Black athlete to suffer such a fate. We do not know what went on in Moon's mind and soul. Could he have been victimized by the tri-headed demon of fame, money, and racial stereotyping?

What we do know is that one evening a news report indicated that Warren Moon was apprehended for stalking and attempting to strangle his wife. Ironically, Moon's wife, who refused to press charges, headed an advocacy group for the protection of abused women. Mrs. Moon supported her husband's statements that she attacked him, and the police dropped the charges. (On February 28, 1996, on Black Entertainment Television (BET), he talked about his role in the conflict. During the interview, Moon appeared to be leaning away from his wife.) Warren Moon and Felicia Fontenot Hendricks were high school sweethearts and married in 1981. His son placed the 911 call about his father attacking his mother. When Felicia Moon recanted her statement and said she was the aggressor (in April 1994), she saved her family, and she saved Warren Moon's football career, paving the way for his entrance into the Hall of Fame. She saved Warren Moon! They subsequently divorced in 2000. Let us give the remarried Felicia Fontanelle props for being the strong, loving, committed, nurturing, and competent (Black) woman every man needs but doesn't always deserve.

Moon talked about his former wife in his Hall of Fame acceptance speech: "I also want to thank the mother of my children, Felicia Fontanelle. She was with me when I was a junior in high school. You couldn't ask for a more supportive, a more loving wife that kept a family together throughout all those years of my professional career. I'm so happy that she's happy in her life right now. I'm so glad that she's here today, because she's as important a part of my career as anybody that's passed through my life. Thank you for being here, Felicia. I'll always love you."

When Warren Moon became embroiled in a physical confrontation with his wife (no matter who started it), it further defined the image of the Black male/athlete as unpredictable and prone to violence. With all due respect to Warren Moon and his family, the pressures of being a Black quarterback caused him to *lose his way.*

While domestic violence seems too epidemic in this country in general, professional and college athletes seem to account for a disproportionate share of it. Research at Northeastern and Massachusetts showed that while White male athletes at thirty division schools made up 3.3 percent of the student body, they accounted for 19 percent of the assaults. What was the message? It was all right for athletes to abuse their girlfriends, as long as they were valuable to the athletic stable. They would be forgiven and allowed to redeem themselves on the athletic field. Or seeing him, wondering what was going through the mind of the girlfriend in those moments she was being abused and terrorized by this fast, strong and angry male. There are, of course, other concerns here, including the victims and the out-of-control athletes. However, the message is that despite all the athletic talent and charitable behavior, the athletes (Black or White) are violent, unpredictable, and their only worth is to channel these generic talents/deficits into a controlled entertainment-oriented environment. Obviously for the social and public view of the athlete, Black or White, it is not enough to say, "I'm sorry; I love you. I'll never do it again"!

While the forces of fame (celebrity), money, and the nagging stereotypes are at work, we should not deceive ourselves by attributing this poor and illegal social behavior solely to an impoverished environment, inadequate parenting, and a criminally oriented peer group. While these factors are important, they should not excuse anyone of the responsibility to act above his or her conditions and not be enslaved by them. Regardless of what happens in life, the most important determinant will be how we respond to it. All of us are ultimately responsible for our behaviors. Before people can heal, they must undergo the process of forgiving themselves and taking responsibility for their behaviors. The best advice we can give to our Black/white athletes and ourselves is to repeat the words "I am responsible!" When you take responsibility, you take back your power. When you blame someone else, you give your power away. Athletes, especially Black athletes (Black people), have endured centuries of having their power taken away. Hey, they should never take their own power away. *They should never lose their own way!*

Basketball great Dick Barnett wrote an article for the *Daily News* (August 13, 1995). Barnett played with the Syracuse Nationals (1959–1961), Los Angeles Lakers (1962-1965), and New York Knicks (1965–1973), winning two NBA championships (1979–1973) with the Knicks. In his article, Barnett decried the numerous incidents of Black athletes' behavior, such as drug abuse, insubordination, and suspensions. He cited the fact that the teams, owners, general managers, and coaches had not come to terms with the realities of the sport, namely race and culture. Many teams had not provided sufficient support and one-on-one experts to relate, communicate, and defuse the athletes' feelings of social isolation. He believed that many athletes had not been able to deal with a society that often stereotyped them as being dangerous. Often the athletes' sudden rise to celebrity did not make them immune to being seen as just another Black man. Barnett said many athletes come from less- than-desirable living circumstances, and that sports are not just a game; they take on "feelings of self-actualization and affirmations of manhood." Barnett wanted sports management to become more sensitive to the traditions, mores, speech-language, music, style of dress, and overall "cool" of Black athletes. He noted that with their paradigm shift from their previous environment, they became disillusioned by the money, the women, and the fame, which had damaging effects on their sports career and their life after sports, and they lost their way!

Dick Barnett was right. While you are supposed to be a grown man at the time you enter professional sports, typically the average age for rookies in football is twenty-two, and it could be as young as eighteen years old. Physically they are grown men, but emotionally and socially, that is far from the truth. Some rookies have a stable support system in place, but many do not have unified families and have no one to guide or support them during this critical period of their lives. Thus, when they encounter the demons of fame, money, and implicit racism, it seldom turns out to be good. Their talent cannot sustain them, and neither can drugs, material things, or women.

VINCENT YOUNG

A PROFESSIONAL SPORTS team's environment and business organization are critical to any player's growth and development, on and off the field. The Houston Oilers/Tennessee Titans seemed to have a toxic working environment in terms of their Black quarterbacks' experiences. Warren Moon received death threats during his tenure. Vince Young (2004) struggled in the organization. Young, the Diet Pepsi Rookie of the Year (2006, two Pro Bowls, 2006 and 2009), left the game because fans booed him over an interception. He suffered a sprained medial collateral ligament after he was coerced and prodded to return to a game. In 2011, Young spent most of his $34 million salary and filed for Chapter 11 bankruptcy, reportedly a result of his excessive spending and the betrayal of his advisors. With all due respect to Vince Young and his family, he was just another Black quarterback who lost his way. As a person and a Black quarterback, Vince Young matters.

STEVE MCNAIR

THE HOUSTON OILERS/TENNESSEE Titans did not treat their greatest quarterback, Steve McNair (February 14, 1973–July 4, 2009), much better. McNair was the Titans' all-time leading passer. He achieved the Associated Press's MVP (2003), three Pro Bowl selections (2000, 2003), and the "Whizzer White" Man of the Year Award (2005). Steve McNair led the Titans to within twelve inches of winning a Super Bowl, and he led them to the playoffs four times. He also served as mentor to Vince Young (1999). His passer rating was 80.1 percent, and he had the third-highest rushing total, 674 yards, for quarterbacks in NFL history. Despite giving his heart and soul to this team, the organization did not respect him. Being locked out of the Titans' training facility, after putting his talent and body on the line and being one their most faithful and successful employees, was unconscionable. The bottom line, however, is no matter what the Titans or the world is like or not like, it was McNair's responsibility not to lose his way, to understand that as a person and a Black quarterback, his life and his families' lives mattered.

McNair was estranged from his wife, Mechelle McNair; the two sons (Tyler and Trenton) he had with her; and his sons, Steve and LaTreal, whom he had with two other women. Tragically, in 2009, McNair became a victim of a suicide-homicide, by his twenty-year-old girlfriend, Sahel Kazemi. For a long time, it appeared that McNair was having personal and family challenges, which no one from his football family seemed to know about. He was not just a football player who was paid big money to play football; he was a person with a family and complex relationships. He needed and deserved more than access to a professional football training facility. With all due respect to Steve McNair and his family, he needed someone to help him, because his life mattered!

JOE GILLIAM

ANOTHER CASE WAS "Jefferson Street" Joe Gilliam (December 29, 1952–December 25, 2000), who played for the Pittsburgh Steelers (1972–1975) and New Orleans Blue Knights (1981) in the NFL and the Washington Federals (1983) in the United States Football League (USFL). Joe Gilliam was selected on the eleventh round of the 1972 draft. He was a two-time All-American at Tennessee State. In 1974, he outperformed Terry Bradshaw and Terry Hanratty to become the starting quarterback and first African-American quarterback to start a season since the AFL-NFL merger. He was featured on the cover of *Sports Illustrated*. Gilliam was 4-1-1 in his first six games before being benched for issues related to performance and not following team rules and game plans. They installed Bradshaw as starting quarterback, and he led the team to the first of four Super Bowl victories. Bradshaw said, "He [Jefferson Street Joe] gave me my job back....It is not like I beat him out."

Joe Gilliam battled heroin, cocaine, and alcohol addiction over the years, and he lived in a cardboard box under a bridge for two years. He was arrested in New Orleans (1976) for possession of a firearm and cocaine. The New Orleans Saints cut him in 1976 and 1977. He played semipro ball for the Pittsburgh Wolf Pack (1978) and the Baltimore Eagles (1979). He also played for the USFL's Denver Gold (1979). Gilliam acquired the nickname Jefferson Street Joe from the boulevard that runs by Tennessee State University in Nashville. Finally, he was inducted into the American Football Association's Semi-Pro Hall of Fame. Some people considered Gilliam to be the Jackie Robinson of Black quarterbacks in modern-day professional football, but there will never be another Jackie Robinson. Gilliam, however, did suffer the explicit racial discrimination and death threats that Robinson experienced.

Jackie Robinson was an amazing Olympic-caliber athlete who starred in basketball, football, track and field, and, his worst sport, baseball. He had the ability to be an Olympic decathlete like Jim Thorpe. Arguably, these two individuals are the two greatest athletes ever produced on American soil. As previously stated, Joe Gilliam was no Jackie Robinson, but he was an amazing quarterback. His arm and the quickness of his release were unbelievable. He was the only quarterback this writer ever witnessed who could carry the football at waist level and fire it at ear level at such speed that his arm was a blur (anyone can confirm this by watching films of him on the internet). Gilliam had a lightning-fast, machine-gun release with the accuracy of a red-laser-equipped sniper rifle. However, he was not as concerned about his football arsenal as he was about the threat of rifles and revolvers being stockpiled to kill him. He allegedly carried a number of weapons to keep himself safe. What was the Steelers organization doing to keep him safe? In addition to arming himself, Gilliam began to chemically fortify himself. He said he used cocaine to deal with the physical pain of playing pro football, but it is also reasonable to assume he found a drug solution to deal with the trauma of being the first Black modern-era starting NFL quarterback. He had no big contract money or fame to deal with; he was fighting to survive the reality of racial animus and racial stereotyping peculiar to being Black and a professional quarterback. We now know that it is a misnomer to say someone has a drug problem; a person has a drug solution. People use drugs to attenuate, to escape from their real problems. Obviously, drugs cause their own problems, making them a poor solution to the individual's real dilemma. With all due respect to Joe Gilliam and his family, he lost his way! The highly gifted Jefferson Street Joe Gilliam transitioned from this life (December 25, 2000) at the age of fifty, and yes, this Black quarterback's life and career mattered.

Jackie Robinson did not use drugs to deal with his stresses. However, the stress took a toll on his physical health and his marvelous athletic body. In 1972, he transitioned from this life at the young age of forty-seven, due to complications from diabetes and cardio problems. What we can say is that Jackie Robinson was a great athlete in baseball, track, and football, and his life definitely mattered!

His wife, Rachel Robinson, said, "I celebrate the progress made in our society and the impact of my partner on those advances…participating in a major movement enhances the belief and investment in social change. However, the most optimistic among us must acknowledge how much remains to be done. However, we must be ever vigilant and active as new facets of prejudice and racial stereotyping appear. Most importantly we need to fight back the forces of retrenchment.…"

MICHAEL VICK

MICHAEL VICK WAS born on June 26, 1980. In college (Virginia Tech, 199–2000), he received the Best College Football Player award in 2000 and the Gator Bowl MVP in 2001. He was the first African-American quarterback ever chosen as the number one pick in the NFL draft (2001). He played six seasons for the Atlanta Falcons and twice led the Falcons to the playoffs. In addition, Vick was named the AP Comeback Player of the Year (2010), played in four Pro Bowls (2002, 2004, 2005, 2010), and earned the Ed Block Courage Award (2009), Archie Griffin Award (1999), and Best NFL Player Award (1999). He was the all-time leading rusher (6,109 yards) for quarterbacks, and his professional football passer rating was an excellent 80 percent. He was a better passer than most people thought.

Michael Vick had the money, the celebrity, and the fame. He was in a city heavily populated with African-Americans. The mayor was African-American, and most of the city council was African-American. Vick had endorsement contracts from Nike, EA Sports, Coca-Cola, Powerade, Rawlings, Hasbro, and Airtran Airlines. Atlantans were rabid sports fans, and they loved a winner. Michael Vick appeared to be that winner. Vick was the man. He was Mr. Excitement on the field. His opponents were in awe of his speed and ability to run the ball out of the quarterback position. He was a bit arrogant, and he often referred to himself in the third person. Michael Vick did not seem to be affected by the stereotypes attributed to Black quarterbacks, although he seemed to run better than he passed. It was almost as if he saw himself as invincible. He generally refused to slide to avoid unnecessary contact, which could place him in danger of injury. At the time, it seemed that Michael Vick was all about Michael Vick. He did not spend the necessary time in the film room, and he did not put in the extra time at practice. He was an extraordinarily gifted football player who made little effort to grow and develop his skill level. He seemed as if he could not be touched by anyone's stereotype or opinion of him. His stresses and downfall could be masterminded only by Michael Vick himself.

Michael Vick chose to deal with the stresses and celebrity of being a Black professional quarterback on his own. He started messing with the canines; literally and figuratively, his life went to the dogs. With all due respect to Michael Vick and his family, he lost his way! As a Black quarterback, a Black male, and a role model, his life matters!

In April 2007, Vick became a person of interest in an illegal dog-fighting ring. In August 2000, he pleaded guilty to federal felony charges and served twenty-one months in prison with two months' home confinement. He lost his Atlanta Falcons/

NFL contract and his product endorsements, and he filed for Chapter 11 in July 2008. He was released by the Atlanta Falcons and signed with the Philadelphia Eagles in 2009. He received the Comeback Player award in 2010. Unlike his predecessors, the stress of racial slurs/stereotypes slid off him as if he was made of Teflon. It was his own judgment, ego, and lack of advisors that caused his trauma, stress, and imprisonment. He lost his way. Fortunately, Michael Vick began to find his way. Because Vick was ready to be a student, Anthony "Tony" Dungy—a moral and religious man, coach, and football player—appeared and became his teacher. He helped Michael Vick to find his way, because the lives of Black quarterbacks matter!

RANDALL CUNNINGHAM

RANDALL CUNNINGHAM IS an exceptional man and NFL quarterback. Although he lost his parents at an early age, he had a family support system. He was resilient, and he eventually found spiritual strength in God. This Black quarterback matters. In Cunningham's case, it was spiritual and religious enlightenment, but it could have been anything that provided internal strength and hop ofsomething better, stronger, and higher than him, something to lean on in those periods of loss, trauma, and stress.

Randall Cunningham's credentials as a man and a quarterback are remarkable. He played in the league for fifteen years: four Pro Bowl selections (1988, 1989, 1990, 1998), Pro Bowl MVP (1998, 1990, 1988), UPI Player of the Year (1990), Comeback Player of the Year (1992), and Eagles Hall of Fame inductee (200). He had a career QB rating of 81.5 percent and a 106 percent passer rating in 1998. He was an outstanding passer, in addition to his ability to extend the play and run the ball when he needed to. His punt average was 44.7 yards (longest 91 yards), and he rushed for 942 yards (1990). He played for the Philadelphia Eagles, Minnesota Vikings, and the Baltimore Ravens. Cunningham performed at a high standard. In 1998, he led the Vikings to a 15-1 record, losing by a field goal in the conference championship game. He was the first celebrity Black quarterback. He did commercials and radio programs, visited children's hospitals, held press conferences, owned an expensive wardrobe, and drove expensive cars. He believed in God and was a team player. In his early years, the media and the fans often misunderstood him. His statistics and amazing performances defined him as an individual who changed the game. He is the best combination and Russell Wilson, RG III, Cam Newton, and Michael Vick. His career passing and running were in the range of Hall of Famer Steve Young. He is currently a pastor, a mentor, a loving husband, and a family man. Maybe someday the Hall of Fame committee will realize who and what they have been missing.

What is most important is that Randall Cunningham, while he never seriously lost his way, found a way through his belief in a higher power. Take away from this what you can; the belief in something or someone greater than yourself has helped many a troubled soul in or outside of sports.

Russell Wilson, Cameron Newton, and Colin Kaepernick are the present generation of significant quarterbacks, Black or otherwise. They have four Super Bowl appearances and one Super Bowl victory among them, and likely more will come. We are watching their greatness and their lives unfold, but they are still criticized for being too "Black" (Cameron Newton), too controversial (Colin Kaepernick), and not being "Black" enough

(Russell Wilson). Others like Tyrod Taylor and Dak Prescott are still unproven. Now there is a new group of rookie quarterbacks in the 2017 season: Deshaun Watson (Clemson University), Patrick Mahomes (Texas Tech), Deshone Kizer (Notre Dame), Brad Kaaya (University of Miami), and Joshua Dobbs (University of Tennessee). They are not struggling under the weight of the Black quarterbacks from the not-so-distant past, but old stereotypes die hard, so we will see. Without question, most Black quarterbacks are men of integrity and high personal values. At the end of the day, these individuals are both Black men and Black quarterbacks, and they matter!

THE N-WORD MATTERS!

THE N-WORD WAS used to label Black quarterbacks, Black athletes, and Black people in general, so the N-Word matters.

> We want this word "NIGGER" to be policed from the parking lot to the equipment room to the locker room. Secretaries, PR people, whoever, we want it eliminated completely and want it policed everywhere.
>
> —John Wooten, Fritz Pollard Alliance

Thanks to the strange relationship between ex-Miami Dolphins' offensive linemen Richie Incognito and Johnathan Martin and the subsequent Bleacher Report, the malevolent word of the day is under attack by representatives of the NFL. Whites have used the N-word to attack Blacks for centuries, and Blacks have used it against other Blacks for almost as long. Usually the

N-word was coupled with the word *Black*, so if one used the phrase "Black nigger" one would be redundant. However, this writer also has heard the terms "white niggers," "red niggers, and "yellow niggers." Apparently, Martin and Incognito frequently used this word in their verbal exchanges, texts, and emails. It is almost incomprehensible that a Black Stanford University graduate would use this word to express himself to anyone. The explanation Martin gave was that Incognito was "an honorary brother." That comment was mindful of what comedian Paul Mooney said in the 2000 film *Bamboozled*. I paraphrase, "White people think it is cool to be Black. If they bring back lynching, they won't think it's so cool [to be Black]." It is all good to hang out and enjoy each other's dress, mores, and culture, but there are places one should not go and lines that should not be crossed. The *nigger* or *nigga* word is that place and that line. Certainly, writers and other artists have used these words for historical accuracy and dramatic effect. Once I tried to support and protect a gay patient from being harassed by some of his Black coworkers. I had the power position of being the Black doctor of this White gay man. He and I had a good one-on-one rapport in our therapy relationship. However, in the group situation (sitting with him and his tormentors), he called me a homophobic nigger.

There is also "the generational effect." Blacks who experienced the pre-civil rights and the civil rights movement are less likely to approve of using the word. Younger generations far removed from the civil rights movement and only intellectually aware (or not) of its history tend to be more accepting of the N-word. Older Blacks regard the use of the N-word as disparaging and denigrating. As a child, I was spit at and called a nigger. As an adult, this writer witnessed a White motivational speaker tell a mainly all-White audience the story of how he had tried to eliminate the negative impact of the N-word to a group of Black professionals. He had them repeatedly sing a jingle—"I'm a nigger...you're a nigger too!"—to change the meaning of the word to something amusing. It did not work! It also did not work for me to listen to his failed attempt as I sat in a mostly White audience. I believe the young White audience had no understanding of the historical impact of the N-word. The younger generation (White or Black) in general does not know what its elders are talking about. Certainly the Black athletes of today are different [but currently we see a retroactive change emerging] from a Tommie Smith or John Carlos of four decades ago. In 1968, two Black men stood on the Olympic podium in New Mexico and raised their fists in the Black power salute, uttering, "To my people be proud." These two Black men were categorically different from many of today's athletes, who have little or no objection to the use of the N-word on the field of play, in the locker rooms, or anywhere else.

The athletes of four decades ago aspired to elevated personal values and a sense of social justice and racial equality. Few can argue with present-day athletes' desire for economic gain and independence, but now they seem to be finding their way. Sadly, since the 1970s, we seem to have lost a generation—or two or three—of young Black men, who have dealt drugs, dropped out of school, randomly killed each other, and superficially identified with their African origins, embracing hip-hop and rap music without really knowing their deeper cultural roots.

THE BLACK QUARTERBACK SOCIAL CHANGE TIMELINE

THIS CHAPTER PRESENTS the counter-argument to the idea that football, and the personnel changes that occur within it, is an end product of social evolution. Sport, including football, is not an entity that changes the culture but is changed by it.

This paper will examine social change and the liberation of football during the last four decades. The incidence of racial equality in society will be used as a measure of social change. More specifically, it will be argued that the increased integration and elevation of Blacks to more professional roles heralded the emergence of the Black athlete as quarterback.

The quarterback position was chosen because its function is analogous to the middle and upper management positions in corporate America. Historically, the quarterback position has been accorded the greatest value on a football team. While football is considered to be a coach's sport, the coach's surrogate on the field is the quarterback (Keidel, 1985).

Participation at the quarterback position enhances the athlete's financial value and greatly facilitates his rise to a higher level of organizational functioning and future financial opportunities. Similarly, the lower value placed on other football positions encumbers the athlete's progress up the organizational ladder and negatively impacts his post-football economic opportunities. The position of quarterback is not only a standard of leadership but also the dividing line between success and failure, on and off the playing field.

Corporations possess many characteristics similar to those present in the organizational structures of collegiate and professional football. In both systems, the athlete-employee encounters the challenge of rising from an entry-level position to one of greater power and importance. This situation is particularly critical in professional sports, where the athlete's opportunity to be employed in an extremely well-paid position is limited by the physical demands of his occupation and the threat of a career-ending injury. Corporate vice presidents and quarterbacks also are similar, to the extent that they each have a modest share of influence and power within their respective organization (Keidel, 1985).

The Black athlete's quest to obtain the status of quarterback is, in substance, no different from the obstacles that Blacks and other minorities faced when they sought corporate middle and upper managerial positions in the late 1960s and the early 1970s (Dickens and Dickens, 1982; Davis and Watson, 1982).

During the '60s and '70s, Black athletes had been clustered in positions that were considered to require only raw athletic talent.

Blacks and other minorities were significantly underrepresented in the positions "requiring" cognitive, decision-making, and leadership skills (Brower, 1972). A survey in *The Physician and Sportsmedicine* (1973) indicated that out of a sample of 1,400 college players, 56 percent of the Black players were running backs, defensive backs, or wide receivers. The positions mentioned were those that were believed to require very little thinking or decision-making ability.

Edwards (1973), Meggyesy (1970), Brower (1972), and Jenkins (1972) have discussed the prevalent beliefs of the 1950s and 1960s, which encompassed the notions that (1) Blacks could not be depended upon, (2) Blacks did not give consistent performance, (3) Blacks did not have the experience or the genetic attributes to excel in leadership roles, and (4) Blacks were instinctive, reflex-oriented athletes. In football terms, these beliefs were translated into a reluctance to groom and develop Black quarterbacks and a tendency to shift Black athletes toward positions that required quick, instinctive reactions.

It was assumed that Blacks did not possess the passing skills or intellectual ability to perform effectively at the quarterback position. If a Black athlete were to compete for the quarterback position, he would have to overcome this stereotype of himself in his own mind and in those of teammates, coaches, and fans. He would have to mount a major psychological campaign to avoid the influence of this negative self-fulfilling prophecy.

In the 1950s, major social changes swept the country, causing classrooms, workplaces, and the athletic fields of America to begin the process of racial integration.

Dr. Ralph Bunche, a Black man, received the Nobel Peace Prize

(1950). Dr. Martin Luther King Jr. led in the Montgomery bus boycott (1957). And the Supreme Court ruled it unconstitutional for several formerly all-white universities and public school systems to practice segregation: Sipuel vs. Board of Regents of the University of Oklahoma (1948), McLaurin vs. Oklahoma State Regents (1950). Sweatt vs. University of Texas (1950), Brown vs. the Board of Education of Topeka (1954), and Bolling vs. Sharp (1955). The desegregation of elementary schools, high schools, and colleges was the foundation from which a number of Black quarterbacks would emerge.

While large-scale integration was just beginning at the collegiate level, Fritz Pollard (Brown, 1916) had already been credited with being the first Black quarterback in professional football and its first Black head coach. In the 1940s, the All-American Football Conference signed George Taliaferro (Indiana, 1949) who became the second Black quarterback in professional football. In 1946 the National Football League admitted its first Black players, Kenny Washington and Willie Strode (both from UCLA). In 1953, the Chicago Bears played Willie Thrower (Michigan State, 1953) at the quarterback position.

In the 1960s, even greater social and political changes took place. The federal courts ordered public schools and universities in the North, South, and Southwest to desegregate. The following list includes the Black students (nonathletes) who were the first to attend formerly all-white institutions: James Meredith (University of Mississippi, 1962), Hamilton Holmes and Charlene Hunter (University of Georgia, 1961–62), and Vivian Malone and James Hood (University of Alabama, 1963).

The passage of the Civil Rights Act (1964) and Elementary

and Secondary School Acts (1965) also set the stage for important social changes. In addition, the March on Washington (1963) and Dr. Martin Luther King Jr. receiving the Nobel Peace Prize (1964) were events of symbolic importance.

In the waning years of the '60s, the Kerner Commission issued its report (1968). The Kerner Commission's report was arguably one of the most important social documents of the latter half of the twentieth century. The Kerner Report identified racial discrimination practices in employment, housing, and welfare and educational systems of our country. The commission strongly recommended changes in the current social-political system, which was creating a separate and unequal white and Black America.

At the close of the '60s, the Metropolitan Applied Research Center compiled a list of Black office-holders (1971). The list included ten members of the US Congress, 173 state legislators, 51 mayors, 701 other city and county officials, 423 school board members, and 228 law enforcement officials (Kaiser, 1971).

Unfortunately, the '60s were marred by widespread violence, which lessened the impact of the massive changes taking place: the assassinations of Malcolm X, Dr. Martin Luther King Jr., President John F. Kennedy, and presidential candidate Robert Kennedy; the Black boycott of the 1968 Olympics; the Black power salute to the American flag during these same Olympics; and the race riots of 1967.

In the midst of the ongoing turmoil, Black athletes were being actively recruited by all the major colleges to play intercollegiate sports. Jerry Levias, wide receiver (SMU, 1964), became the first Black to play in the Southwest Conference (SWC), followed by

Greg Page (Kentucky, 1965), the first Black football player in the Southeastern Athletic Conference (SEC).

During the same time frame, Ernie Davis (Syracuse, 1961) became the first Black player to win the Heisman Trophy, designating him as the most outstanding college football player. Mike Garrett (1965) and O. J. Simpson (1968) of Southern California also won the Heisman award, but Davis, Garrett, and Simpson were not quarterbacks.

It was the installation of the option offense in college football that increased the opportunity for Blacks to play quarterback and demythologized the quarterback position. Major college teams were recruiting and "converting" more Black athletes to play the option quarterback position. The option attack, whether it was the wishbone, the split T, or the veer, were ground-oriented offenses with the quarterback being essentially another ball carrier. In the option offense, the quarterback's role was either to run the ball himself or hand off the ball laterally to a trailing running back. Option quarterbacks, Black or White, had to be good runners, but they were usually mediocre; thus, the stigma remained about Blacks being unable to be "real" quarterbacks.

Despite the greater opportunity to play quarterback, the only place a Black athlete could be supported and nurtured as a quarterback was at the traditionally Black colleges and the Canadian Football League. Grambling College and Tennessee State University were the first Black quarterback "factories," producing James Harris, Matt Reed, Doug Williams, and Joe Gilliam Jr. These athletes were all effective "passing" quarterbacks, who enjoyed better-than-average success in professional football. Generally, those Black quarterbacks from predominantly white schools were shifted to other positions in the professional ranks. Many of these quarterbacks had to travel to Canada in order to play quarterback at the professional level.

The following is a partial listing of Black collegiate quarterbacks who played in the 1960s: (1) Willie Wood (Southern California, 1960); (2) Peter Hall (Marquette, 1961); (3) Wilburn Hollis (Iowa, 1961); (4) Sandy Stephens, first Black consensus All-American quarterback (Minnesota, 1961); (5) Mike Howell (Grambling, 1965); (6) Brig Owens (Cincinnati, 1966); (7) Jim Plunkett (Stanford, 1966), first nonwhite quarterback to win the Super Bowl—he won two Super Bowl rings playing for the then Oakland Raiders; (7) Carroll Williams (Xavier, 1966); (8) Hank Washington (West Texas State, 1966); (9) Eldridge Dickey (Tennessee A&I, 1966); (10) Eddie McAshan (Georgia Tech, 1967–71); (11) Marlin Briscoe (Omaha, 1967); (12) James Harris-MVP, 1975 Pro Bowl (Grambling, 1967); (13) Garry Lyle (George Washington, 1967); (14) Jimmy Raye (Michigan State, 1969); (15) Karl Douglas (Texas A&I, 1970); (16) Jimmy Jones (Southern California, 1971); (17) Chuck Ealey (Toledo, 1971); and (18) Matt Reed, WFL Championship (Grambling, 1972).

Although the 1970s saw a slowing of social progress outside the sports area, baseball appointed Frank Robinson (1974) as its first Black manager (Cleveland Indians), and approximately thirty-five Blacks were hired as assistant coaches in the National Football League. Lenny Wilkins, Al Attles, and K. C. Jones obtained head coach jobs in professional basketball. Wayne Embry and Elgin Baylor were former basketball players who became vice presidents and general managers in professional basketball. This acceleration of Blacks into higher management in professional baseball and basketball brought additional pressure on professional football to consider qualified Blacks for head-coach positions. However, it was not until 1989 that the National Football League's Oakland Raiders appointed Art Shell. It was also in the late eighties when Bill White was appointed as a major-league baseball commissioner.

The conservative social climate of the 1970s was symbolized by the Supreme Court's Bakke Decision (1978). The Bakke Decision made it unconstitutional to "reserve" positions for minorities in graduate schools or the job market. Despite the Bakke case, more Blacks were attending and graduating from formerly segregated schools and achieving professional career goals. Major colleges continued to recruit Black athletes who had good leadership qualities and passing ability; Condredge Holloway (Tennessee, 1972) signed as the SEC's first Black quarterback. Bear Bryant's Alabama team signed Wilbur Jackson (1970) as its first Black running back; eventually Alabama recruited Walter Lewis (1982) as its first Black quarterback.

The following is a partial listing of Black quarterbacks of the 1970s and 1980s, many of whom became successful professional quarterbacks either in the United States or in Canada: (1) Condredge Holloway (Tennessee, 1974) played quarterback in Canada; (2) John Walton (Elizabeth City State University, 1970) played three years with the Philadelphia Eagles; (3) Doug Williams (Grambling, 1974), Tampa Bay and Washington Redskins MVP, Super Bowl 1988; (4) Parnell Dickerson (Mississippi Valley State, 1976) played one year with Tampa Bay; (5) David Mays (Texas Southern, 1976) played three years with Cleveland and in Buffalo; (6) Vince Evans (Southern California, 1977) played the backup quarterback with the Chicago Bears and the Oakland

Raiders; (7) Warren Moon (University of Washington, 1978), Canada and the Houston Oilers; (8) Walter Lewis (Alabama, 1982), USFL; (9) Randall Cunningham (UNLV, 1985), Philadelphia Eagles; (10) Reggie Collier (Southern Mississippi 1980), USFL; (11) Tracy Ham (Georgia Southern), drafted by the Rams, shifted to kick returner, now playing quarterback in Canada; (12) Rodney Peete (USC, 1989), Detroit Lions; (13) Don McPherson (Syracuse, 1987), the second Black consensus, All-American quarterback; (14) Jamelle Holieway (Oklahoma, 1989), quarterbacked the 1985 National Championship team; (15) Major Harris (West Virginia, 1986–90), playing in Canada; (16) Tony Rice (Notre Dame, 1989), second Black quarterback on a National Championship team; (17) Reggie Slack (Auburn, 1989); and (16) Andre Ware (University of Houston, 1989), first Black quarterback to win the Heisman Trophy, first-round draft choice of the Detroit Lions.

The following is a complete listing of Blacks who have won the Heisman award, only two of whom played quarterback at the college or professional level: Jim Plunkett (Stanford, 1970), at least one publication listed Jim Plunkett's parents as Mexican-Americans, but the media never classified him as being Black. There seems to be little doubt, however, that he was the first non-White quarterback to win the Heisman Trophy and two Super Bowls; Johnny Rodgers (Nebraska, 1972); Archie Griffin (Ohio State, 1974); Archie Griffin (Ohio State, 1975); Tony Dorsett (Pittsburgh, 1976); Earl Campbell (Texas, 1977); Billy Sims (Oklahoma, 1978); Charles White (USC, 1979); George Rogers (South Carolina, 1980); Marcus Allen (USC, 1981); Herschel Walker (Georgia, 1982); Michael Rozler (Nebraska, 1983); Bo Jackson (Auburn, 1985); Tim Brown (Notre Dame, 1987); Barry

Sanders (Oklahoma State, 1988); and Andre Ware (Houston, 1989).

Despite the number of Black players who had won the coveted Heisman Trophy in the 1960s and 1970s, it was not until the late '80s that people truly believed the Black quarterback had arrived. Three Black quarterbacks were selected as leading candidates for the Heisman Trophy, with the Heisman being won by Andre Ware, who set a new college passing record. To place this event in its proper perspective, please review the events in the entire updated timeline.

TIMELINE OF SOCIAL CHANGE AND THE CHANGES IN FOOTBALL

SOCIAL CHANGE	CHANGE IN FOOTBALL
1920-1949 – No Civil Rights Legislation passed – dominated by Jim Crow legislation.	*1920* – Fritz Pollard (Brown, '16) first Black quarterback and head coach in professional football (APFA)
1948 – Sipuel v. Board of Regents of The University of Oklahoma	*1946* – Kenny Washington and Willie Strode – First Black players in the NFL (both from UCLA, '46)
1941 – Seven NYU students, "The Bates Seven" were suspended for three months for protesting against the University's discrimination against its Black star fullback Leonard Bates, by refusing to let him play against an all-White University of Missouri football team.	*1949* – George Taliaferro (Indiana, '49) 2nd Black quarterback in professional football (AAFC)

SOCIAL CHANGE	CHANGE IN FOOTBALL
1950 – Ralph Bunch received the Nobel Peace Prize	*1953* – The Chicago Bears played Willie Thrower (Michigan State, '53) at the quarterback position
1950 – Sweatt v. University of Texas	*1957* – Prentice Gautt, (Oklahoma, '61) first Black player in the Big 8 Conference
1950 – McLaurin v. Oklahoma State Regents	
1954 – Plessy v. Ferguson	
1954 – Brown v. The Board of Education of Topeka	
1955 – Bolling v. Sharp	
1957 – Dr. Martin Luther King leads in the Montgomery Bus boycott	
1961 – Desegregation of the University of Georgia	*1961* – First Black quarterbacks to play in the Big Ten. Wilburn Hollis (Iowa '61); Sandy Stephens (Minnesota, '61) – first Black QB Consensus All-American
1962 – Desegregation of the University of Alabama	*1961* – Ernie Davis, RB (Syracuse, '61), first Black to win the Heisman Trophy
1962 – Desegregation of the University of Mississippi	*1964* – Jerry Levias, WR (SMU, '68), first Black to play in the Southwest Conference

SOCIAL CHANGE	CHANGE IN FOOTBALL
1963 – Assassination of President Kennedy	*1965* – Greg Page (Kentucky, '69), became the first Black football player in the Southeastern Conference (SEC)
1964 – Dr. Martin Luther King received the Nobel Peace Prize	*1965* – Heisman awarded to running backs Mike Garrett (1965) and O.J. Simpson (1968) of Southern California
1964 – Passage of the Civil Rights Act	*1967* – Eddie McAshan, first Black QB in the ACC, (Georgia Tech, '71)
1965 – The assassination of Malcolm X	*1969* The Black "14" fourteen Black football players University of Wyoming University dismissed for protesting racial discrimination at Brigham Young University
1965 – Passage of the Elementary and Secondary Schools Act	
1967 – Race riots in Urban America	
1967 – Bill Russell named first Black player-coach of the Boston Celtics Basketball team	
1968 – Assassination of Robert Kennedy	
1968 – The Kerner Commission Report	
1968 – The Black Athletes' Boycott of the 1968 Olympics	
1968 – Assassination of Dr. Martin Luther King	
1970s – Lenny Wilkins, Al Attles, K.C. Jones obtained head coaching jobs in professional basketball	*1970* – Advent of the Wishbone Option Offense in college football

TIMELINE OF SOCIAL CHANGE AND THE CHANGES IN FOOTBALL

SOCIAL CHANGE	CHANGE IN FOOTBALL
1970s – Wayne Embry and Elgin Baylor were former basketball players, vice-presidents and general managers in professional basketball	**1970** – Jim Plunkett (Stanford, '70) – first Mexican-American QB to win the Heisman Award
1970s – Approximately 35 Blacks were hired as assistant coaches in the National Football League	**1972** – Condredge Holloway (Tennessee, '76), first Black QB in the SEC
1974 – Frank Robinson appointed first Black manager (Cleveland Indians)	**1972** – Heisman Trophy awarded to (receiver-kick returner) Johnny Rodgers University of Nebraska
1978 – "Bakke Decision"	**1974** – Joe Gilliam (Tennessee State, '72) first Black QB to start on Monday Night Football
	1974 – Heisman Trophy awarded to running back Archie Griffin of Ohio State University
	1975 – James Harris (Grambling, '72) QB; MBP 1975 Pro Bowl
	1975 – Heisman Trophy awarded to running back Archie Griffin of Ohio State University
	1976 – Matt Reed (Grambling, '72) QB; WFL – Championship Quarterback
	1976 – Heisman Trophy awarded to running back Tony Dorsett University of Pittsburg
1984 – Jesse Jackson ran for President of the United States	**1980** – Jim Plunkett (Stanford, '70) QB MVP Superbowl XV

SOCIAL CHANGE	CHANGE IN FOOTBALL
1988 – Jesse Jackson ran again for President of the United States	**1980** – Heisman Trophy awarded to running back George Rogers University of South Carolina
1989 – NFL's first Black head football coach – Art Shell of the Los Angeles Raiders	**1981** – Heisman Trophy awarded to running back Marcus Allen University of Southern California
1989 – A Black mayor elected in New York City	**1982** – Heisman Trophy awarded to running back Herschel Walker, University of Georgia
1989 – A Black governor elected in Virginia	**1983** – Jim Plunkett (Stanford, '70) QB Superbowl XVIII Championship team
1989 – Orenthal James Simpson pleaded no contest to charges of spousal abuse	**1983** – Heisman awarded to running back Mike Rosier, University of Nebraska
	1985 – Heisman Trophy awarded to running back Bo Jackson Auburn University
	1987 – Don McPherson (Syracuse, '87) 2nd Black QB consensus All-American Quarterback
	1987 – Heisman Trophy awarded to running back Tim Brown, University of Notre Dame

SOCIAL CHANGE	CHANGE IN FOOTBALL
	1988 – Doug Williams (Grambling, '74) QB Tampa Bay and Washington Redskins) MVP, Superbowl XXII
	1988 – Tony Rice (Notre Dame, '89) first Black QB for a National Championship Team
	1988 – Heisman Trophy awarded to running back Barry Sanders, Oklahoma State University
	1989 – Andre Ware, (University of Houston, '89) first Black QB to win the Heisman Trophy
1991 – *Anita Hill testified that Supreme Court Justice Nominee Clarence Thomas, sexually harassed her while he was he was her supervisor at the Department of Education and the EEOC*	**1991** – Heisman Trophy awarded to receiver/kick returner Desmond Howard, Michigan University
1994/6/12 – *People of the State of California v. Orenthal James Simpson (murder trial)*	**1992** – Heisman Trophy awarded to Quarterback Charlie Ward, Florida State University
1996 – *The parents of Ron Goldman filed civil suits against Orenthal James Simpson (civil trial) for wrongful death suit and a "survivor suit."*	**1994** – Heisman Trophy awarded to Rashaan Salaam Running Back, University of Colorado
	1995 – Heisman Trophy awarded to running back Eddie George, Ohio State University

SOCIAL CHANGE	CHANGE IN FOOTBALL
	1997 – Heisman Trophy awarded to defensive back/receiver Charles Woodson, University of Michigan
	1998 – Heisman Trophy awarded to running back Ricky Williams, University of Texas
	1999 – Heisman Trophy awarded to Ron Dayne running back, University of Wisconsin
2001/9/11 – The Twin Towers fell under the weight of the attack of two airliners hijacked by Al-Qaeda terrorists. America was now at war with Iraqi and Afghanistan.	2003 – Marcus Allen inducted into the Pro Football Hall of Fame- 1981 Heisman Trophy,USC –SUPER BOWL XVIII MVP- 1985 NFL MVP
2008 – Barack Obama elected as the first Black President of the United States.	2006 – Heisman Trophy awarded to Quarterback Troy Smith, Ohio State University
2012 – Barack Obama won re-election for President of the United States.	2007 – Tony Dungy First African-American coach to a NFL Super Bowl (XLII)
2012 – Alicia Garza, Patrisse Cullors, and Opal Tometi created and founded #BlackLivesMatter in response to George Zimmerman being acquitted of the shooting death of 17- year-old Trayvon Martin.	2009 – Heisman Trophy awarded to running back Mark Ingram .Jr. University of Alabama

SOCIAL CHANGE	CHANGE IN FOOTBALL
2014 – Sexual assault allegations against comedian Willian Henry Cosby Jr. (Bill Cosby) by over sixty women, dating back over several decades.	2010 – Heisman Trophy awarded to Quarterback Cameron Jerrell Newton Quarterback, Auburn University
2014 – Ray Rice, running back (Baltimore Ravens) arrested and subsequently indicted for third-degree assault on his fiancée.	2011 – Heisman Trophy awarded to Quarterback Robert Griffin III, Baylor University
2014/8/9 – Unarmed teenager Michael Brown killed by a white police officer on the sidewalks of Ferguson, Missouri. Violence began with looting and destroying of businesses. The police responded with riot gear and military weapons. The scenes played out over national and international media, and the President was troubled by the event and the Ferguson community's response to the event. Community protests and marches took place across the United States.	2013 – Heisman Trophy awarded to Quarterback James Winston Florida State University, after being criminally cleared of sexual assault charges
2016/7/11 – Allegedly in response to the recent police shootings, Mica Xavier Johnson ambushed a group of police offices in Dallas, Texas. He killed five officers, wounded nine others along with two civilians, before Johnson was contained and neutralized.	2014 – Russell Wilson Quarterback (University of Wisconsin/Seattle Seahawks) leads Seattle to XLVIII Super Bowl win over the Denver Broncos

SOCIAL CHANGE	CHANGE IN FOOTBALL
2016/8/4 – In Baton Rouge, Louisiana, Gavin Long shot and killed three police officers and wounded three others. Long's suicide note said, "My attack was a necessary evil' in the hope that good cops would weed out the bad cops and stop the violence being imposed on 'my people.'"	**2015** – Heisman Trophy awarded to running Derrick Henry University of Alabama
2016 – San Francisco Forty-Niner quarterback Colin Kaepernick sat and eventually knelt for the playing of the National Anthem.	**2015** – Cameron Jerrell Newton Quarterback (Auburn University/ Carolina Panthers) named NFL Most Valuable Player
2016 – The New York Times published the article " Crossing the Line: How Donald Trump behaved with women in private." President Trump accused of sexual assault and sexual harassment by at least fifteen women since the' 80s.	**2016** – Heisman Trophy awarded to Quarterback Lamar Jackson University of Louisville

SOCIAL CHANGE	CHANGE IN FOOTBALL
2017 – Newly elected President Donald Trump believed the protest was against the American flag and the National Anthem and called on the NFL to fire the players. The truth is the protest was about the increasing number of people of color being violently assaulted and often killed by the police, including but not limited to Trayon Martin, Sandra Bland, Freddie Gray, Alton Sterling, Philando Castile, and Michael Brown.	
2017/11/28 – NFL player representatives and league officials reached agreement for the league to provide financial support to players' community activism initiatives. The agreement did not address player protests during the national anthem	
2017 – Sexual harassment allegations levied against Representative Tim Murphy; Representative Blake Farenhold; Representative Ruben Kihuen , Representative John Conyers, Jr. ,Senator Al Franken, and Roy S. Moore, Republican Senate candidate (Alabama).	

SOCIAL CHANGE	CHANGE IN FOOTBALL
2017 – Roy S. Moore defeated in his run for Senate seat, mainly due the voting of Black women in Alabama and the rise of the #MeToo cultural shift of sexually assaulted female victims.	
	2018 Heisman Trophy awarded to Quarterback Kyler Murray of the University of Oklahoma

BLACK YOUTH RACISM AND SPORTS

RECENTLY, BLACK ATHLETES have spoken out against the idolization of athletes by disadvantaged youth and the thinking that sports are an easy way to success. The reasons why young people are so easily seduced by this idea is the prevalence of professional sports and athletes in the mass media and statements like this:

"Sport in recent years has opened some very special doors. Every male Black child, however he might be discouraged from a career with a Wall Street brokerage firm, knows he has a sporting chance in baseball, football, boxing, basketball or track. He might even make it in other sports....The Black youngster has something real to aspire to when he picks up a baseball bat or dribbles a basketball."

The above quote is from Martin Kane, former senior editor for *Sports Illustrated*. Mr. Kane, in his article, attempts to emphasize athletics as the one true avenue of success for the Black male. While it is true that many Blacks have achieved success through sports, it is a grievous mistake to direct our Black youth into this area. It is the purpose of this discussion to demonstrate that Blacks find it just as difficult to succeed in athletics as they would in any other occupation.

All young people begin with dreams of succeeding in our society. America's work ethic says that no matter who you are, you can succeed in this land of opportunity. Many a young person, White and Black, has experienced the pain of frustration when they begin to test their dreams against reality. The fallacy of the land-of-opportunity concept and self-doubt about the future may be the keys to understanding the personality traits and problems of our youth today. The Black youth has been encouraged to get ahead, only to find his or her goals unobtainable. Blacks in America constantly find their pursuit of success interfered with by an entrenched system of racial discrimination, no matter what occupational goals they wish to attain. Black youth remain isolated from the American dream because America is not what most people think of it as: a classless society. For Blacks, America functions as a caste system, and it is difficult to leave the low status they have been born into. Most other immigrants came to America with the options of marrying out of their status or waiting until their children became "Americanized." Blacks have no such options, since marrying out of their race is generally frowned upon, and their children would still be considered Black, no matter what level they attain.

No one would deny that America is a very sports-minded country. In fact, the embodiment of our moral character was exemplified by the athlete. The clean-living, crew-cut, all-American boy was the image that fathers wanted for their sons. Today, professional and amateur athletes are idolized by the youth of America. Most American males have been sold the idea that the one true goal in life is to make it as an athlete. That is why most fathers buy sports equipment for their newborn sons; the father sees his second chance to attain athletic glory through his son.

The identification factor and vicarious experience components account for the big-business aspect of spectator sports in the United States. It is not just a team you're watching win or lose, but *your* team. The success or failure of the team becomes *your* success or failure.

The advertising media have not lost sight of what sports and sports heroes mean to America, and consequently Madison Avenue has used athletes to market products. On television and radio, athletes (mostly White) sell everything from soda pop to deodorant.

In fact, many professional athletes make more money doing commercials than they do during the season. Mark Spitz never made a nickel from swimming, but after winning seven gold medals in the 1972 Olympics, he was offered $3 million in commercial endorsements. Decathlon champion Bruce Jenner has also received many lucrative offers. It is interesting to speculate whether a Black athlete winning seven gold medals would be offered such large sums of money. Certainly we know that Milton Campbell and Rafer Johnson—Blacks who won the gold medal in the decathlon—were not able to cash in on their title of "the World's Greatest Athlete."

It is without question that even Black athletes are made highly visible in the mass media and that, coupled with the availability of playgrounds, would make sports seem a logical way of "making it." Here would be a chance of making more money and having more prestige and attention than one would be likely to achieve in another career or a blue-collar job.

What the Black youth should not forget is racism is so deeply embedded in our society that nowhere can he escape its restrictive and degrading effects. No matter how good a ballplayer he is, or thinks he is, there is always someone better. And in spite of public statements to the contrary, most college and professional teams use a quota system. This quota system ensures that only so many Blacks will be on the team, field, or court. The method normally used is called *stacking*, which involves Black athletes going out for the same few positions, while other positions are reserved for White athletes.

A survey in *The Physician and Sports Medicine* (1973) indicated that out of a sample of 1400 college players, 56 percent of the Black players were running backs, defensive backs, or wide receivers. The positions mentioned are believed to require very little thinking or decision-making ability. These positions basically require instinctual reactions, at which, it is believed, Blacks excel (pp. 1–15).

The so-called thinking positions that require intellect and decision-making—center, offensive guard, and quarterback—had only 4 percent of the Black players. It is not unusual to have this kind of breakdown on any integrated team, and most coaches would honestly admit that they were unaware of what they were doing (pp. 1–15).

The situation at quarterback is particularly infuriating in its racist intent. If another survey were taken today, the quarterback situation would have a much higher percentage of Blacks. The greater number of Blacks playing quarterback in collegiate football is not due to social change or enlightenment but to the shift to the Texas wishbone offense or the Houston veer offense. In both of these offensive setups, the quarterback essentially becomes another halfback and uses his speed and quick reactions to make each play successful. There is very little passing, play calling, or thinking associated with either of these attacks, and this may explain why coaches are no longer reluctant to have Black quarterbacks.

The implied reasons behind the professional game's reluctance to use Blacks at quarterback are (a) Blacks can't be relied on under pressure, (b) Blacks are not good leaders, (c) Blacks are not intelligent enough, and (d) Blacks play so much better at other positions. Most people familiar with the study of mankind know that the characteristic of leadership is not exclusively owned by Whites, nor does it require a mental giant to read defenses and memorize plays. In fact, most players are required to learn the team's playbook, and defensive backs must learn to think along with the quarterback so they have an idea of the type of play they must defend against.

To this observer, the qualities a professional quarterback should have are (a) a strong throwing arm, (b) peripheral vision, (c) good size, (d) mobility, and (e) leadership. Although there are those who would deny it, color also seems to play a part in the qualities a pro prospect must possess. If this were not true, why is so much made over the fact that a player making his debut as a pro quarterback is Black and no reference to race is made when the player is White?

An example of this was the case of Joe Gilliam (Tennessee State '71). Gilliam was to make his debut with the Pittsburgh Steelers against the then-World Champion Miami Dolphins. In front of a national television audience, under the pressure that he was representing the hope of his people and that his success would prove there is no genetic truth to the idea that Blacks are less intelligent than Whites, the tragedy that befell Gilliam—two early pass interceptions leading to easy scores for the Dolphins—could have been predicted. The miracle of Gilliam's situation was that he was given the opportunity to apprentice as a professional quarterback and not shifted to another position.

It usually takes three to four years for a college quarterback to understand the professional game well enough to play competently. When a Black quarterback is drafted, he usually is assigned a different position and/or told he will be given an "opportunity" to play quarterback. As time passes, the Black rookie begins to experience the frustration attendant to learning the quarterback position. Additionally, he is told that he is too good an athlete to be wasting his time sitting on the bench and that he could help the team more by being a defensive back or a wide receiver. Most White prospects are not subjected to this type of treatment, partly because their general athletic ability is such that the only position they could play, professionally, is quarterback.

In 1966, two Black quarterbacks, Henry Washington (West Texas State) and Eldridge Dickey (Tennessee State), insisted that they be given a legitimate chance to be quarterbacks when drafted. Dickey was drafted by the Oakland Raiders, played quarterback in some exhibition games (hardly the three-year incubation period needed by most quarterbacks), and was then switched to wide receiver. Later Dickey was traded to the Kansas City Chiefs and labeled a troublemaker and difficult to handle. (These are the usual terms coaches give players who challenge their authority or question their judgment; these labels are usually your ticket out of professional football.) After a brief stay with the Chiefs, Eldridge Dickey—a superb athlete, fine pass receiver, and a man of strong beliefs—was not heard of again.

The late Hank Washington's case was a little different. Washington was a known quantity, and his passing record spoke for itself. He had an arm like a bazooka, and, as some would have you believe, a mouth like a machine gun. On the eve of one of the many post-season all-star games he was to appear in, Washington demanded to be drafted as a quarterback, stating that quarterback was the only position he would play. Indeed, Washington, like many of his White counterparts, would have been too slow to play anywhere else. In the 1967 professional draft, of the twenty-six teams then in existence none saw fit to draft Henry Washington.

Perhaps, however, the greatest case of racial injustice inflicted on a Black quarterback took place at the collegiate level. For three years, Edward McAshan (Georgia Tech '72) survived the pressures of playing quarterback at a formerly all-White university. Just attending and graduating from Georgia Tech would have been a great achievement, but also to start at quarterback and lead his team to the Sun Bowl ('71) and the Liberty Bowl ('72) proved that Eddie was an outstanding individual. McAshan's excellent throwing motion and high rating in the collegiate passing statistics suggested that he would be a high draft choice as a quarterback.

In McAshan's senior year, Eddie wanted some extra tickets so his family and relatives could see him play his final game for Georgia Tech (not an uncommon request from star athletes). His request was refused, and justifiably hurt and confused, McAshan stayed away from practice. Coach William Fulcher suspended McAshan for conduct detrimental to the team, the charge carrying with it the subtle label of troublemaker. What a fitting way for Georgia Tech to give thanks to Eddie McAshan. His presence had brought national attention to that university, as well as a winning record (20-12-1)—not to mention the revenue in gate receipts and television money.

So there was Edward McAshan, suspended, uninvited to any of the all-star games, and drafted on the *last round* by the New England Patriots. At the time of the McAshan draft, the Patriots already had a young quarterback who had won the Heisman Trophy in 1970. Most critics agreed that Jim Plunkett, having completed his third year of apprenticeship, would reach superstardom as a professional quarterback. Plunkett, the son of blind parents (one Mexican and the other Black), was usually referred to as being Mexican-American and rarely as being Afro-American; thus, the pressures of debuting as a Black quarterback did not apply to him. As of the 1977 season, Plunkett is still a starting quarterback, but he has yet to achieve the stardom predicted for him.

A partial listing of Black collegiate quarterbacks and what happened to them is as follows: (1) Willie Wood (Southern California '60) was not drafted but later became an all-pro safety with the Green Bay Packers. (2) Peter Hall (Marquette '61) shifted to wide receiver for the New York Giants. (3) Wilburn Hollis (Iowa '61) played quarterback in Canada. (4) Sandy Stephens (Minnesota

'61) played quarterback in Canada. (5) Mike Howell (Grambling '65) was shifted to defensive back by the Cleveland Browns. (6) Brig Owens (Cincinnati '66) was shifted to defensive back by the Washington Redskins. (7) Carroll Williams (Xavier '66) played quarterback in Canada. (8) Marlin Brisco (Omaha '67) was drafted as a defensive back, but due to an emergency, the Denver Broncos allowed him to play quarterback. After a brilliant rookie season, Brisco was traded and shifted to wide receiver (where he made all-pro). Brisco currently plays wide receiver for the New England Patriots. (9) James Harris (Grambling '67) was the only Black quarterback given the full opportunity to play the position, due to the foresight of the Buffalo Bills. Harris is the starting quarterback for the San Diego Chargers. (10) Garry Lyle (George Washington '67) was shifted to halfback and then to safety by the Chicago Bears. (11) Jimmy Jones (Southern Cal. '71) went to Canada, where he is playing quarterback. (12) Chuck Ealey (Toledo '71) went to Canada, where as a rookie he led his team to the championship title. (13) Matt Reed (Grambling '72) was shifted to linebacker and tight end by the Denver Broncos and then cut from the team. Reed later played quarterback in the World Football League and led his team to the championship. Reed is currently playing quarterback in Canada. (14) Condredge Holloway (Tennessee '74) is playing quarterback in Canada. (15) Vince Evans (Southern Cal. '77) is playing backup quarterback with the Chicago Bears.

While this is not a full listing of all Black quarterbacks of the modern era, it is a listing of those who met the qualifications previously listed for quarterback, with the exception of their being Black. The bottom line seems clear: regardless of the racism that may also exist in Canada, a Black candidate for quarterback is given a competitive chance to play at that position. The idea that one needs great intellectual skills to play quarterback in the United States is purely erroneous and racist in intent.

Presently, the coaches call a large majority of the plays. Frank Ryan (Cleveland Browns) and Charley Johnson (Denver Broncos) were the only playing quarterbacks with doctoral degrees. Neither Ryan nor Johnson was cited for great intellectual acumen on the playing field, but rather, for athletic ability.

In this writer's opinion, Dan Jenkins, a senior editor at *Sports Illustrated*, has written the most tragiccomic paragraphs on racism in professional sports in his book *Semi-Tough*:

"Never give the ball to a nigger on third and three when you're behind and need the yardage. Goddamn it, they'll dog it on you every time. It's too bad they've been raised that way, in Africa, Brazil and Philadelphia and Detroit and everywhere, but that's the way it is. One of these days when they've educated themselves better and shown some…initiative at inventing things like—oh, I don't know, the offshore rig or a diamond drillin' bit, or something useful—then…you can give a nigger the ball on third and three. But not now…I just wouldn't trust a nigger to make a big play for me anymore than I'd trust a spick to fix a flat tire" (p. 109).

The above sentiments were basically the way most major southern colleges felt up until the late '60s and early '70s. On October 20, 1973, this writer had the occasion to watch a game between Tennessee and Alabama on national television. Tennessee was behind in the game, but the team was still in good position to win, thanks to the spirited play of Tennessee's key Black players: quarterback Condredge Holloway and halfback Haskel Stanback.

Suddenly, Alabama tailback Wilbur Jackson turned right end and cut across field on his way to a game-breaking, eighty-yard touchdown.

The most fascinating factors were that Jackson was also Black and that this was no science-fiction scenario but stark reality! Tennessee and Alabama were relying on Black players and using them on national television? Incredible! Simply incredible! The conversation in the press box went something like this:

Duffy Daugherty: "Jackson is the reason why Big Ten football is not as strong as it used to be. All these great Black athletes are staying home and playing ball for these great southern universities."

Bud Wilkinson: "Yes, that's how sports lead the way for society. It doesn't matter what color you are but just how well you play."

While none of these remarks were intended to be racist, hopefully the television audience understood them in the spirit in which they were intended. In fact, there are not two men of higher character and integrity than Duffy Daugherty and Bud Wilkinson. But former Coaches Daugherty and Wilkinson should have known better. In no case has a Black athlete been enrolled at a previously all-White institution without a great deal of opposition from the society at large. Let us not forget that schools like Tennessee and Alabama legally should have started to desegregate as early as 1954 (Supreme Court decision in the case of Brown v. Board of Education, Kansas).

Bud Wilkinson, then coach at the University of Oklahoma (1956), recruited Prentice Gautt to play for him. Coach Wilkinson only needs to reflect back on the trials and tribulations that Gautt must have suffered at the hands of (a) campus society, (b) his fellow players, (c) other teams, (d) classmates, and (e) his professors just for the right to become the first Black to play for Oklahoma and the Big Eight Conference. Surely Coach Wilkinson was not unaware of the Supreme Court decisions in the cases of Sipuel v. Board of Regents of the University of Oklahoma, 1948, and McLourin v. Oklahoma State University, 1950 (*Afro USA*, pp. 17–243), which paved the way to the successful desegregation of Oklahoma's institutions of higher learning.

As for the University of Alabama, Coach Daugherty's statement brought to mind the illusion of a great egalitarian society where Blacks could go to school in their home states if they chose to do so. Intruding on these thoughts of sublime fantasy was the image this writer had seen on television years before. Governor Wallace of Alabama (1963) stood in the doorway of the University of Alabama, blocking the admission of Viviane Malone and James A. Hood. There stood Governor Wallace, his face tight and grim, aided by state troopers and National Guardsmen. He didn't give a damn whether a Wilbur Jackson could run eighty yards for a touchdown or not. It was only after the late President Kennedy federalized the Alabama National Guard that Governor Wallace relented and allowed the university to be desegregated. All of this was in contrast to the governor's smiling face on November 17, 1973, when he crowned Terry Points as Alabama's first Black campus queen, who by poetic justice should have been Viviane Malone!

On the evening of November 3, 1973, two more teams were engaged in combat. Louisiana State University was dismantling the University of Mississippi. Late in the game, Coach Voight put in sophomore halfback James Reed. Reed did not turn the game around for Mississippi, but his presence did make the contest interesting. The sports announcers began to focus in on Reed:

"James Reed, born in Meridian, Mississippi, runs the hundred in 9.7 seconds. Man, that's fast!"

On November 17, 1973, Mississippi beat Tennessee, and the architects of the victory were James Reed and Benjamin Williams (Black defensive end). For their efforts, scholarships were donated to the University of Mississippi. As before, the viewing audience was treated to a press box conversation suggesting that in the area of social integration, sports could lead the way. Again, such discourse conjures up earlier memories of the University of Mississippi. In the fall of 1962, Governor Ross Barnett personally refused to admit James Meredith to the university, even after the federal court had ordered his admission. Federal marshals had to escort Meredith to the campus. In the days that followed, violence broke out resulting in two deaths and numerous injuries. Again, President Kennedy had to call out the federal troops and federalize the Mississippi National Guard to restore order. Governor Barnett continued to insist that President Kennedy's action was unconstitutional. Thus, it wasn't sports that led the way to the desegregation of the University of Mississippi but rather a small, Black ex-airman looking for a quality education.

As alluded to earlier, the method that holds back many Blacks from full participation in professional sports is the quota system. Many well-meaning people are convinced that a quota is necessary to ensure a championship team, because a team of all Blacks could never win it all. Again, I quote from Dan Jenkins's *Semi-Tough*:

"A team with seven spooks could make the playoffs and a team with nine spooks could get into the Super Bowl. But a team with ten spooks or more probably couldn't beat Denver" (p. 5).

Wilt Chamberlain said that official quotas may have to be instituted in professional basketball because White fans will not accept all-Black teams (with the exception of the Globetrotters, which many people consider a minstrel show). This writer has often wondered what goes through a White father's head when he sees his son dribbling a basketball between his legs and saying, "Look, Dad, I'm Walt Frazier!" He may be thinking, "The devil you are, son; you're Pete Maravich!"

During the 1970 basketball season, the Atlanta Hawks consistently fielded an all-Black starting five. The players knew and the Atlanta Hawks management feared that if the situation continued, the fans would not support the team. Now it just so happened that this was Pete Maravich's senior year at Louisiana State University, where Pete managed to break Oscar Robertson's all-time career scoring mark. The Hawks promptly drafted Maravich, as they felt that his scoring and showmanship would remedy the club's sagging attendance figures (bring the White fans back). Maravich, in fact, was the only White player ever offered a chance to play with the Globetrotters. Atlanta fans would be happy if Pete could just break up what had become the Atlanta Globetrotters.

Walt Hazard (former UCLA All-American) expressed concern about Maravich's presence in terms of adjusting to Pete's playing style and having to play behind him. The objection was that Pete should have to win a starting berth on the basis of his ability and not because he was White. The press and club management played down the racial overtones of the resentment against

Maravich. The players didn't resent him personally but that he was being used as the tool to "desegregate" the starting five. The newspapers tried to defuse the situation by attributing the conflict to the team having to adjust to Pete's helter-skelter brand of basketball rather than Maravich having to "blend" in with the team.

Two years later, when things had cooled down in Atlanta, a small article appeared in the papers stating that Walt Hazard had been traded. One wonders what would have happened to Hazard if he had not become verbal about the situation, but as the system goes, Hazard would still have been traded. The question that lingers is "Why didn't Hazard continue his career with another NBA team?" Could it be that he had become disgusted and disillusioned with pro sports (thinking that all one has to do is be better than the next guy in order to play, but that only applied if the next guy is the same color as you), or was he put on one of those unofficial blacklists for the act of being a man and speaking his mind?

Finally, let's take the case of Muhammad Ali, which demonstrates clearly how seriously America takes its professional sports and the images their athletes should project. Once Ali allied himself with the Muslims, even his position as heavyweight champion of the world did not make him immune to racism. The coup de grâce came when Ali refused to enter the armed forces for religious reasons. In a move unprecedented in sports annals, Ali's crown was taken from him. The shocking aspect of this was the overwhelming public approval of his political dethronement. The amount of courage it took for Ali to make his decision cannot be estimated. With no "great white hope" waiting in the wings, Ali was the perfect hero for Blacks and Whites alike. His light skin, clean features, and entertainer's sense of moment virtually guaranteed him millions of dollars in commercial endorsements and personal appearances.

After many trying years, Ali was able to regain his crown and make millions of dollars in the process. Ali, however, would be the first to say that while professional sports had been good to a few Blacks of exceptional ability, a good education and proper career training offered the best chance of success for the masses of Blacks and Whites.

Hopefully, the new message is being heard. Sports are a way of succeeding in society but certainly not the *only* way, nor the *best* way, for the Black youth of America.

BIBLIOGRAPHY

Ashe, Arthur, Jr. *A Hard Road to Glory: A History of the African-American Athlete Since 1946.* New York: Warner Books, Inc., 1988.

Board of Education, City of New York. *The Negro in American History, New York, N.Y.* Board of Education Printing Office, 1976, 140–143.

Branch, Taylor. *Parting the Waters: American in the King Years: 1954-63.* New York: Simon and Schuster, 1988.

Brower, J. J. "The Black Side of Football: The Salience of Race," unpublished dissertation. University of California, Santa Barbara, 1972.

Davis, George, and Glegg Watson. *Black Life in Corporate America: Swimming in the Mainstream.* New York: Anchor Press/

Doubleday, 1982.

Dickens, Floyd Jr., and Jacqueline B. Dickens. *The Black Manager: Making It in the Corporate World*. New York: AMACOM, 1982.

Django Unchained, directed by Quentin Tarantino (2012). The Weinstein Company and Sony Pictures Releasing (International). Stars: Jamie Foxx, Christopher Waltz, Leonardo DiCaprio, Kerry Washington, Samuel L. Jackson, Walton Goggins, Dennis Christopher, James Remar, Michael Parks, and Don Johnson.

Edwards, Harry. "The Black Athlete: 20th Century Gladiators for White America," *Psychology Today*, vol. 7 (November 1973): 43–52.

"Football in Black and White," *The Physician and Sportsmedicine*, vol. 1 (June 1973): 15.

Gray, John. *Men Are from Mars, Women Are from Venus*. New York: Harper Collins, 1992.

Hardesty, Von. *Black Wings*. New York: Harper Collins, 2008, 3–119.

Hinton, E., Earnest Reese, and David Davidson. "Run for Respect: a Study of Black Football Players in the South," *The Atlanta Journal-Constitution*, September 7, 1986.

Hollander, Zander, ed. *The Complete Handbook of Pro Football*. New York: Signet Printing, 1990, 214–250.

Holman, Lynn. *Black Knights*. Gretna, LA: Pelican Publishing Company, 2001, 15–50.

Hutchinson, Earl. *The Assassination of the Black Male Image*. New York: Simon & Schuster, 1994.

Jenkins, Dan. *Semi-Tough*. New York: Atheneum Press, 1972.

Jones, Michael Curtis. *Black Son Rising*. Chicago: African American Images, 2006.

Kaiser, Ernest, and Harry Ploski, eds. *Afro USA*. New York: Bellwether Publishing Company, Inc., 1971, 242–243.

Kane, Martin. "An Assessment of Black is Best." *Sports Illustrated*, vol. 34 (January 1971): 72–76.

Kennedy, Randall. *Nigger*. New York: Pantheon Books, 1954.

Klein, Larry, ed. *College Football Modern Record Book*. New York: National Collegiate Sports Services, 1972, 33.

Keidel, Robert. *Game Plans: Sports Strategies for Business*. New York: E. P. Dutton, 1985, 1–76.

Low, Augustus W., and Virgil Clift, eds. *Encyclopedia of Black America*. New York: Da Capo Press, 1988, 228–271.

Mandingo, directed by Richard Fleischer (1975). Paramount

Pictures. Stars: James Mason, Susan George, Perry King, Lillian Hayman, Richard Ward, Brenda Sykes, and Ken Norton.

Murrell, A. J., and E. M. Curtis. "Causal Attributions of Performance for Black and White Quarterbacks in the NFL: A Look at the Sports Pages." *Journal of Sport and Social Issues*, vol. 18, no. 3 (August 1994): 224–233.

Niven, David. "Race, Quarterbacks, and the Media: Testing the Rush Limbaugh Hypothesis." *Journal of Black Studies,* vol. 35, no. 5 (May 2005): 684–694.

Ploski, Harry A. and Ernest Kaiser, eds. *The Negro Almanac.* New York: Bellwether Publishing Company, 1971, 482–549.

Riffenburgh, Beau, and David Boss. *Great Ones.* New York: Viking Press, 1989, 160–165.

Sterkenburg, Van J. and A. Knoppers. "Dominant Discourses about Race/Ethnicity and Gender in Sport Practice and Performance." *International Review for the Sociology of Sport,* 39 (2004): 301. DOI: 10.1177/1012690204045598.

Treat, Roger. *The Official Encyclopedia of Football, Eleventh Revised Edition.* New York: A. S. Barnes and Co., Inc., 1973.

US Riot Commission Report. Report of the National Advisory Commission of Civil Disorders. New York: Bantam Books, 1968.

CPSIA information can be obtained
at www.ICGtesting.com
Printed in the USA
LVHW081352100719
623675LV00028B/378/P